PINK FLOYD
THE DARK SIDE OF THE MOON

50ᵉ ANNIVERSAIRE

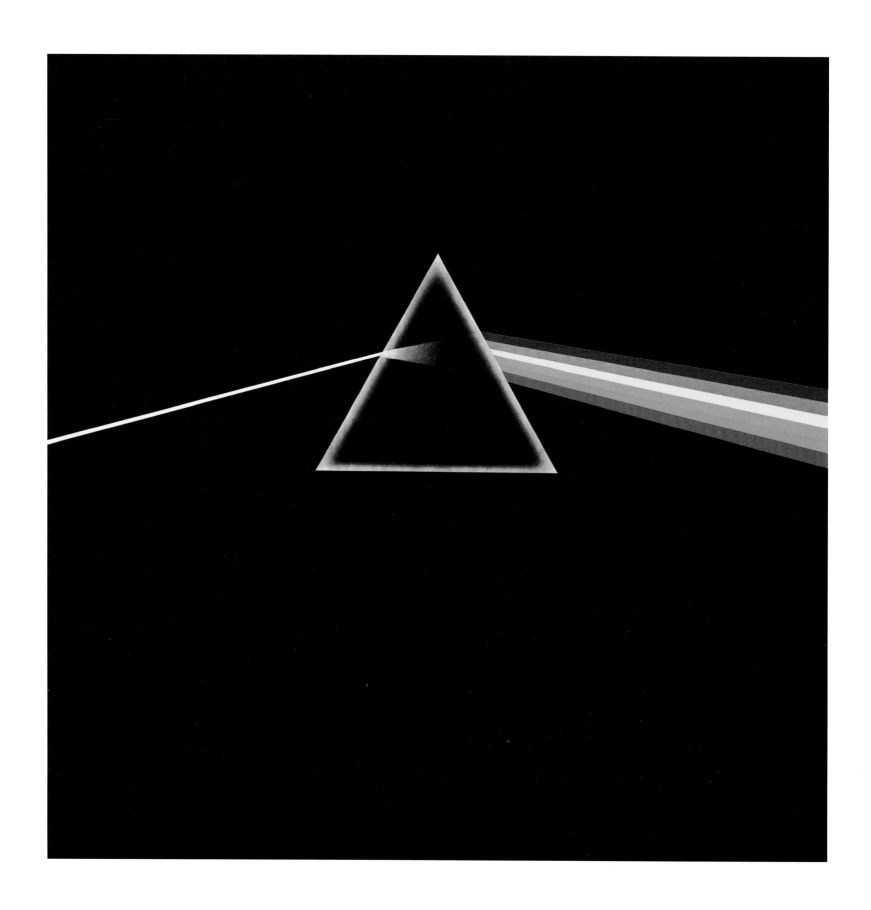

PINK FLOYD
THE DARK SIDE OF THE MOON

50e ANNIVERSAIRE

« Il n'y a pas de face sombre à la lune.
En fait, tout est sombre. »

Gerry O'Driscoll, portier aux studios Abbey Road

cardinal

CAUGHT IN THE ACT

WHILE a host of current bands are injecting glamour and excitement back into rock, the Pink Floyd continue in their own way to do just the opposite. Messrs Waters, Wright, Gilmour and Mason would no sooner wear a satin jacket as finish their set with a rock medley. It's the way it should be, for the Floyd are an institution in this country and elsewhere. They are the world's number one underground band.

And while there are nowadays many who attempt to emulate their space voyage ideas, none are half as good as the Floyd in top gear. They needed no warming up at the Empire Pool,, Wembley, on Saturday. From the word go, they gave the packed stadium a faultless demonstration of what psychedelic music is all about. There wasn't a note, or a sound, out of place during the whole evening.

It's a recital more than a concert, and the Floyd don't so much give us numbers as perform pieces of music, lasting up to an hour each.

For starters on Saturday we had that lengthy work entitled "The Dark Side of the Moon", an eerie title for an equally eerie piece of music that takes the listener through a host of different moods, most of which are accompanied by unusual sounds stretching around his head by way of the group's quadraphonic sound system. I can't understand why more group's don't try this Floydian tactic: the effect is really stunning.

The second half of the recital was composed of three more major pieces, and a couple of encores. The first encore — the riveting "Set The Controls For the Heart of the Sun" — was obviously rehearsed, but the second — a bluesy jam — wasn't. It served a useful purpose to show that the group are not confined to playing science fiction soundtrack music all the time.

The incendiary gimmicks from the stage frequently obliterated the artists. Flasbombs erupted here and there at well-timed places, and Roger Waters' gong actually became a blazing sun during "Controls".

All the time the group were effectively illuminated by their imposing lighting tower at the rear of the stage which served a dual purpose -- at frequent intervals it belched out smoke which mingled with the coloured lights and the dry ice surface mist to effectively wisk us all away to Planet Floyd.

Dave Gilmour is an underestimated guitarist. That he knows his instrument back to front is never really in doubt, but playing guitar with the Floyd demands an extra precision, and the ability to strike harsh chords one minute and lighter notes the next. And he has to be the handiest man around when it comes to using an echo chamber, as the extended notes proved.

R.ck Wright, I suspect, contributes considerably more than just keyboards. Someone must dabble around with pre-recorded tapes and Wright seems to be the obvious choice. Both tape and keyboard work is executed with the unassuming precision that typifies the band's approach to their highly individual music.

One final thought: wouldn't it be great if, for once, they dropped the image and played "See Emily Play" — just for an encore.— CHRIS CHARLESWORTH.

PINK FLOYD: world's number one underground band

Floyd's space odyssey

JOHN SMITH ENTERTAINMENTS
BY ARRANGEMENT WITH STEVE O'ROURKE PRESENT

PINK FLOYD
ON TOUR

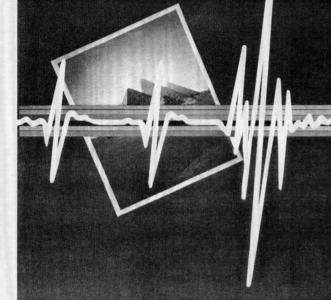

November 4th 1974	Usher Hall, Edinburgh.
5th	
November 8th 1974	Odeon, Newcastle-upon-Tyne.
9th	
November 14th 1974	Empire Pool, Wembley.
15th	
16th	
November 19th 1974	Trentham Gardens, Stoke-on-Trent
November 22nd 1974	Sophia Gardens, Cardiff.
November 28th 1974	Empire Theatre, Liverpool.
29th	
30th	
December 3rd 1974	Hippodrome, Birmingham.
4th	
5th	
December 9th 1974	Palace Theatre, Manchester.
10th	
December 13th 1974	Hippodrome, Bristol.
14th	

All concerts are at 7.30 in the evening except Wembley—
Wembley evening concerts are at 8.00

Extra Date: November 17th Empire Pool, Wembley, 6 p.m.

TICKETS ACCEPTED BY MAIL ORDER ONLY UNTIL 7th OCTOBER
LIMITED TO FOUR TICKETS PER PERSON.

SEND STAMPED ADDRESSED ENVELOPE TOGETHER WITH POSTAL
ORDER TO PINK FLOYD CONCERT AT THEATRE BOX OFFICES.

The Dark Side Of The Moon
Dates de tournée 1972–1975

TOURNÉE BRITANNIQUE, 1972

20 JANVIER
The Dome, *Brighton*

21 JANVIER
Guildhall, *Portsmouth*

22 JANVIER
Winter Gardens, *Bournemouth*

23 JANVIER
Guildhall, *Southampton*

27 JANVIER
City Hall, *Newcastle Upon Tyne*

28 JANVIER
City Hall, *Leeds*

3 FÉVRIER
Locarno Ballroom, *Coventry*

5 FÉVRIER
Colston Hall, *Bristol*

10 FÉVRIER
De Montfort Hall, *Leicester*

12 FÉVRIER
City Hall, *Sheffield*

13 FÉVRIER
Empire Theatre, *Liverpool*

17 au 20 FÉVRIER
Rainbow Theatre, *Londres*

TOURNÉE JAPONAISE, 1972

6 et 7 MARS
Tokyo-To Taiikukan, *Shibuya*

8 et 9 MARS
Place des festivals, *Osaka*

10 MARS
Dai-Sho-Gun Furitsu Taiikukan, *Kyoto*

13 MARS
Centre des sports de Nakanoshima,
Sapporo

ROYAUME-UNI, 1972

29 et 30 MARS
Free Trade Hall, *Manchester*

TOURNÉE NORD-AMÉRICAINE, 1972

14 AVRIL
Fort Homer W. Hesterly Armory, *Tampa*

15 AVRIL
Hollywood Sportatorium,
Pembroke Pines

16 AVRIL
Township Auditorium, *Columbia*

18 AVRIL
Atlanta Symphony Hall, *Atlanta*

20 AVRIL
Syria Mosque Theater, *Pittsburgh*

21 AVRIL
Lyric Theater, *Baltimore*

22 AVRIL
Civic Theatre, *Akron*

23 AVRIL
Music Hall, *Cincinnati*

24 AVRIL
Allen Theatre, *Cleveland*

26 et 27 AVRIL
Ford Auditorium, *Détroit*

28 AVRIL
Auditorium Theatre, *Chicago*

29 AVRIL
Spectrum Theater, *Philadelphie*

1er et 2 MAI
Carnegie Hall, *New York*

3 MAI
John F. Kennedy Center for the
Performing Arts, *Washington*

4 MAI
Music Hall, *Boston*

EUROPE, 1972

18 MAI
Deutschlandhalle, *Berlin-Ouest,
Allemagne de l'Ouest*

ROYAUME-UNI, 1972

28 et 29 JUIN
The Dome, *Brighton*

TOURNÉE NORD-AMÉRICAINE, 1972

8 SEPTEMBRE
Municipal Auditorium, *Austin*

9 SEPTEMBRE
Music Hall, *Houston*

10 SEPTEMBRE
McFarlin Auditorium, *Dallas*

11 SEPTEMBRE
Memorial Hall, *Kansas City*

12 SEPTEMBRE
Civic Center Music Hall, *Oklahoma City*

13 SEPTEMBRE
Henry Levitt Arena, *Wichita*

15 SEPTEMBRE
Community Center Arena, *Tucson*

16 SEPTEMBRE
Golden Hall, *San Diego*

17 SEPTEMBRE
Big Surf, *Tempe*

19 SEPTEMBRE
University of Denver Arena, *Denver*

22 SEPTEMBRE
Hollywood Bowl, *Los Angeles*

23 et 24 SEPTEMBRE
Winterland Auditorium, *San Francisco*

27 SEPTEMBRE
Garden Auditorium, *Vancouver*

28 SEPTEMBRE
Memorial Coliseum, *Portland*

29 SEPTEMBRE
Hec Edmundson Pavilion, *Seattle*

30 SEPTEMBRE
Garden Auditorium, *Vancouver*

ROYAUME-UNI, 1972

21 OCTOBRE
Wembley Empire Pool, *Londres*

TOURNÉE EUROPÉENNE, 1972

10 et 11 NOVEMBRE
K.B. Hallen, *Copenhague, Danemark*

12 NOVEMBRE
Ernst-Merck-Halle, *Hambourg,
Allemagne de l'Ouest*

14 NOVEMBRE
Philipshalle, *Düsseldorf,
Allemagne de l'Ouest*

15 NOVEMBRE
Sporthalle, *Böblingen,
Allemagne de l'Ouest*

16 et 17 NOVEMBRE
Festhalle, *Francfort, Allemagne de l'Ouest*

28 NOVEMBRE
Palais des sports, *Toulouse, France*

29 NOVEMBRE
Parc des expositions, *Poitiers, France*

1er et 2 DÉCEMBRE
Centre sportif de l'Île-des-Vannes,
Paris, France

3 DÉCEMBRE
Parc des expositions, *Caen, France*

5 DÉCEMBRE
Forest National, *Bruxelles, Belgique*

7 DÉCEMBRE
Palais des sports, *Lille, France*

8 DÉCEMBRE
Parc des expositions, *Nancy, France*

9 DÉCEMBRE
Hallenstadion, *Zurich, Suisse*

10 DÉCEMBRE
Palais des sports, *Lyon, France*

TOURNÉE NORD-AMÉRICAINE, 1973

4 MARS
Dane County Memorial Coliseum, *Madison*

5 MARS
Cobo Arena, *Détroit*

6 MARS
Kiel Opera House, *Saint-Louis*

7 MARS
International Amphitheatre, *Chicago*

8 MARS
Armory Fieldhouse, *Cincinnati*

10 MARS
Memorial Gymnasium, *Kent*

11 MARS
Maple Leaf Gardens, *Toronto*

12 MARS
Forum de Montréal, *Montréal*

14 MARS
Music Hall, *Boston*

15 MARS
Spectrum Theater, *Philadelphie*

17 MARS
Radio City Music Hall, *New York*

18 MARS
Palace Theater, *Waterbury*

19 MARS
Providence Civic Center, *Providence*

22 MARS
Hampton Coliseum, *Hampton*

23 MARS
Charlotte Park Center, *Charlotte*

24 MARS
Municipal Auditorium, *Atlanta*

ROYAUME-UNI, 1973

18 et 19 MAI
Earls Court, *Londres*

TOURNÉE NORD-AMÉRICAINE, 1973

17 JUIN
Saratoga Performing Arts Center, *Saratoga Springs*

18 JUIN
Roosevelt Stadium, *Jersey City*

19 JUIN
Civic Arena, *Pittsburgh*

20 et 21 JUIN
Merriweather Post Pavilion, *Columbia*

22 JUIN
Buffalo Memorial Auditorium, *Buffalo*

23 JUIN
Olympia Stadium, *Détroit*

24 JUIN
Blossom Music Center, *Cuyahoga Falls*

25 JUIN
Convention Center, *Louisville*

27 JUIN
Jacksonville Coliseum, *Jacksonville*

28 JUIN
Hollywood Sportatorium, *Pembroke Pines*

29 JUIN
Tampa Stadium, *Tampa*

EUROPE, 1973

12 OCTOBRE
Olympiahalle, *Munich, Allemagne de l'Ouest*

13 OCTOBRE
Wiener Stadthalle, *Vienne, Autriche*

ROYAUME-UNI, 1973

4 NOVEMBRE, 17 h et 21 h
Rainbow Theatre, *Londres*

TOURNÉE FRANÇAISE, 1974

18 JUIN
Parc des expositions, *Toulouse*

19 JUIN
Parc des expositions, *Poitiers*

21 JUIN
Parc des expositions, *Dijon*

22 JUIN
Théâtre de plein air, Parc des expositions, *Colmar*

24 AU 26 JUIN
Palais des sports, *Paris*

BRITISH WINTER TOUR, 1974

4 et 5 NOVEMBRE
Usher Hall, *Édimbourg*

8 et 9 NOVEMBRE
Odeon, *Newcastle Upon Tyne*

14 au 17 NOVEMBRE
Wembley Empire Pool, *Londres*

19 NOVEMBRE
Trentham Gardens, *Stoke-On-Trent*

22 NOVEMBRE
Sophia Gardens Pavilion, *Cardiff*

28 au 30 NOVEMBRE
Empire Theatre, *Liverpool*

3 au 5 DÉCEMBRE
Birmingham Hippodrome, *Birmingham*

9 et 10 DÉCEMBRE
Palace Theatre, *Manchester*

13 et 14 DÉCEMBRE
Bristol Hippodrome, *Bristol*

TOURNÉE NORD-AMÉRICAINE, 1975

8 AVRIL
Pacific National Exhibition Coliseum, *Vancouver*

10 AVRIL
Seattle Center Coliseum, *Seattle*

12 et 13 AVRIL
Cow Palace, *San Francisco*

17 AVRIL
Denver Coliseum, *Denver*

19 AVRIL
Tucson Community Center, *Tucson*

20 AVRIL
University Activity Center, *Tempe*

21 AVRIL
Sports Arena, *San Diego*

22 au 27 AVRIL
Los Angeles Memorial Sports Arena, *Los Angeles*

7 JUIN
Atlanta Stadium, *Atlanta*

10 JUIN
Capital Centre, *Landover*

12 et 13 JUIN
Spectrum Theater, *Philadelphie*

14 JUIN
Roosevelt Stadium, *Jersey City*

16 et 17 JUIN
Nassau Veterans Memorial Coliseum, *Uniondale*

18 JUIN
Boston Garden, *Boston*

20 JUIN
Three Rivers Stadium, *Pittsburgh*

22 JUIN
County Stadium, *Milwaukee*

23 et 24 JUIN
Olympia Stadium, *Détroit*

26 JUIN
Autostade, *Montréal*

28 JUIN
Stade Ivor-Wynne, *Hamilton*

ROYAUME-UNI, 1975

5 JUILLET
Knebworth Park, *Stevenage*

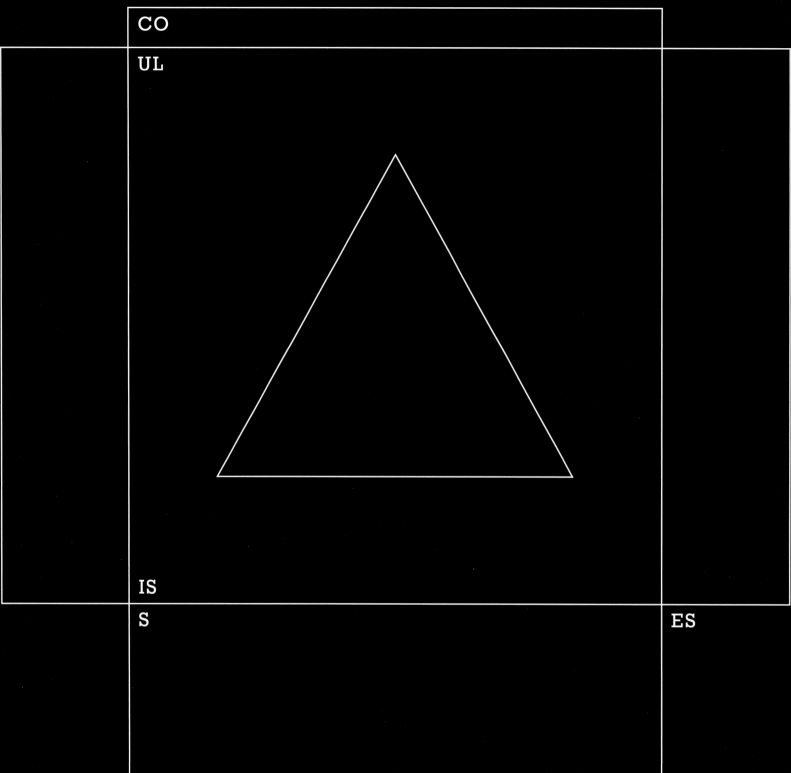

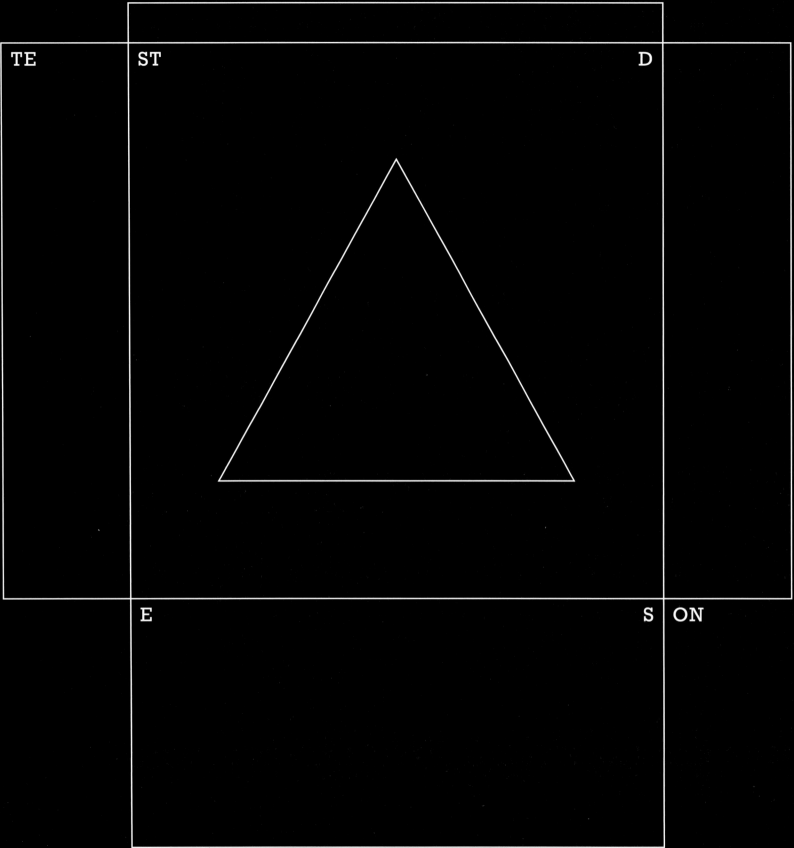

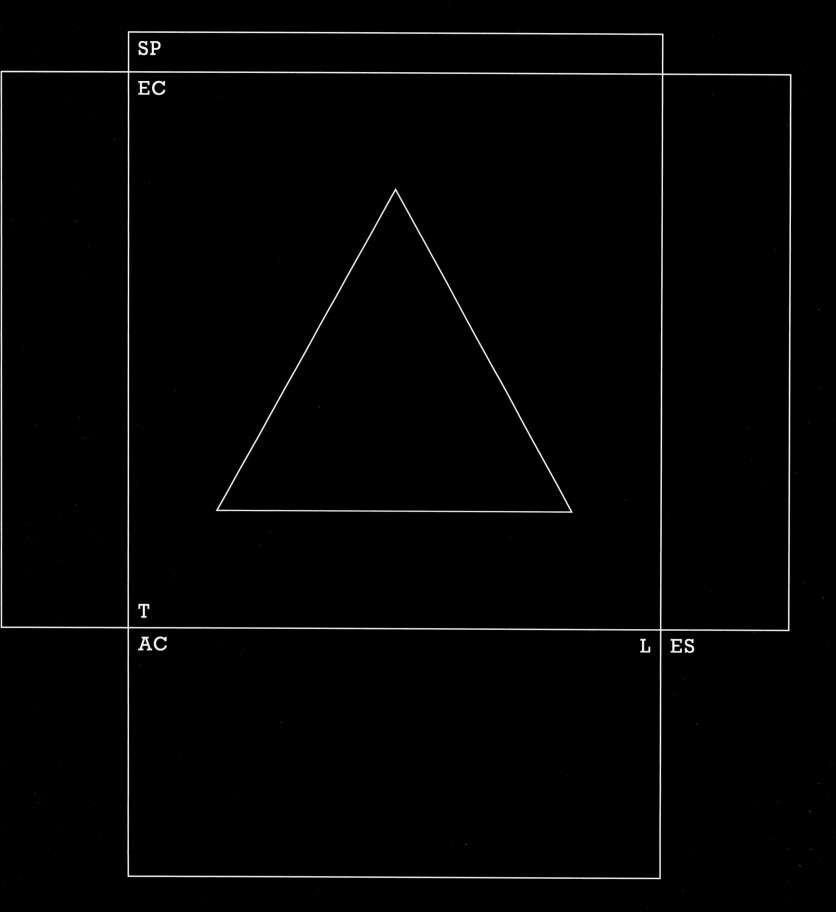

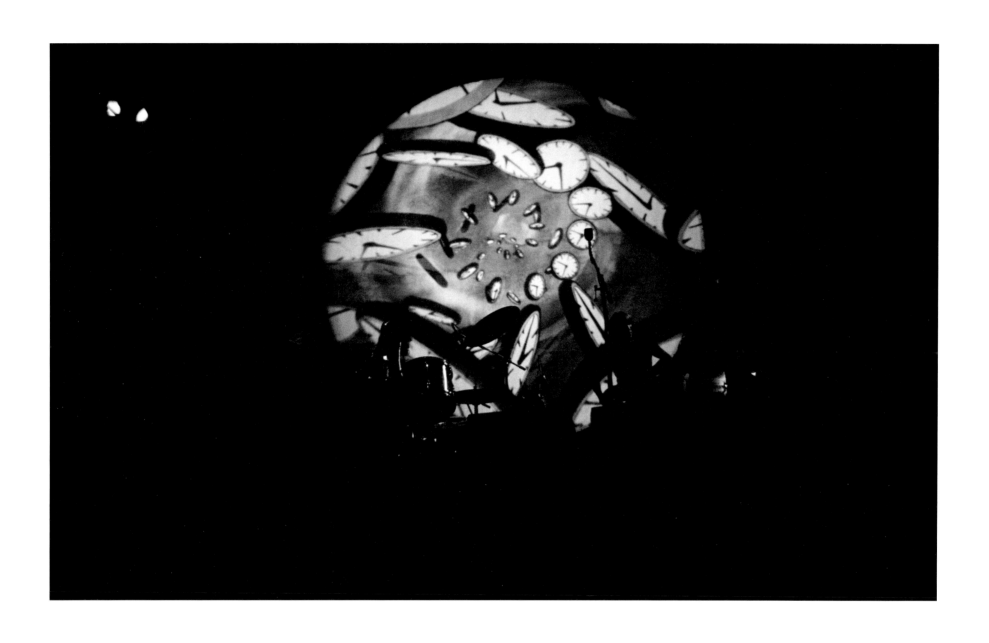

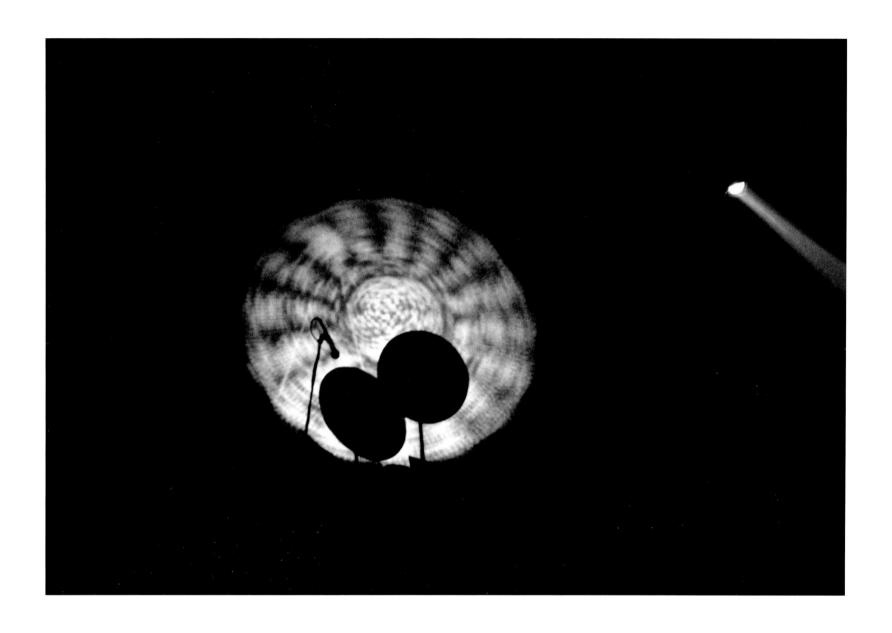

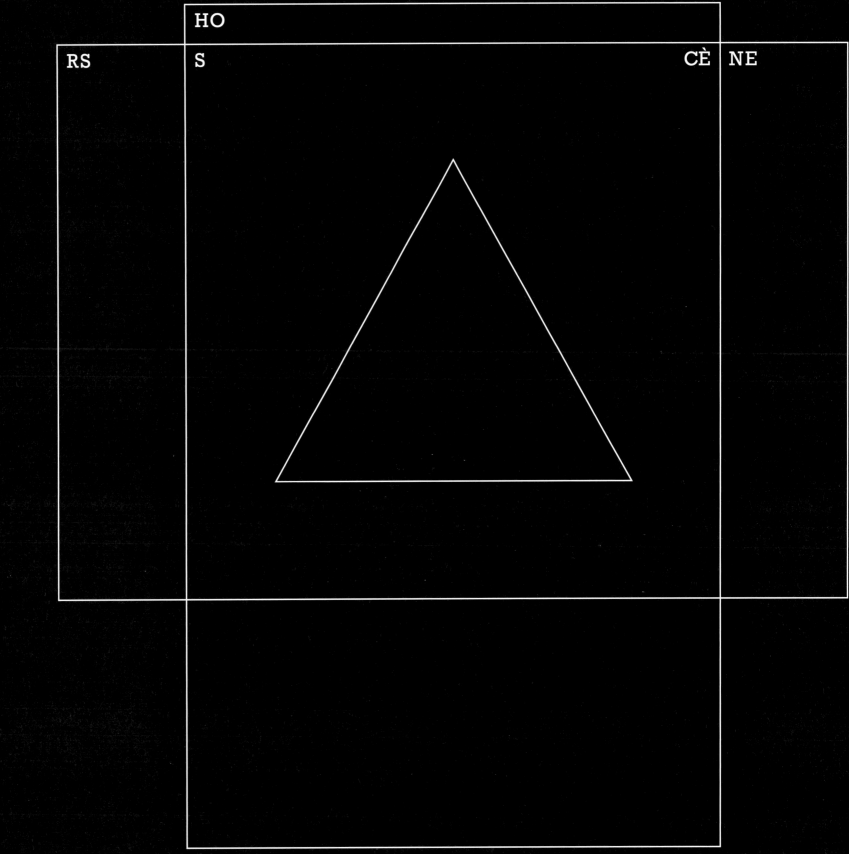

VI
SU
EL
S

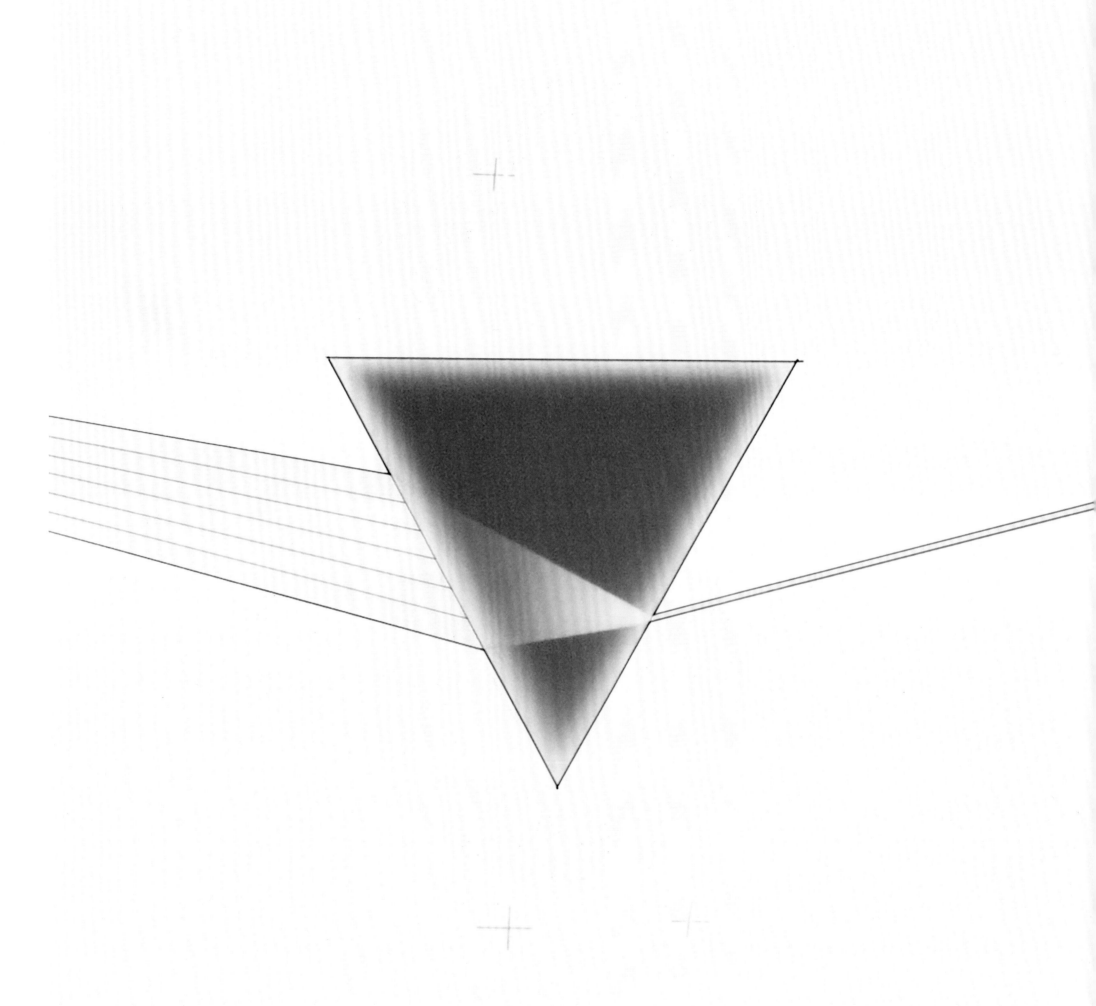

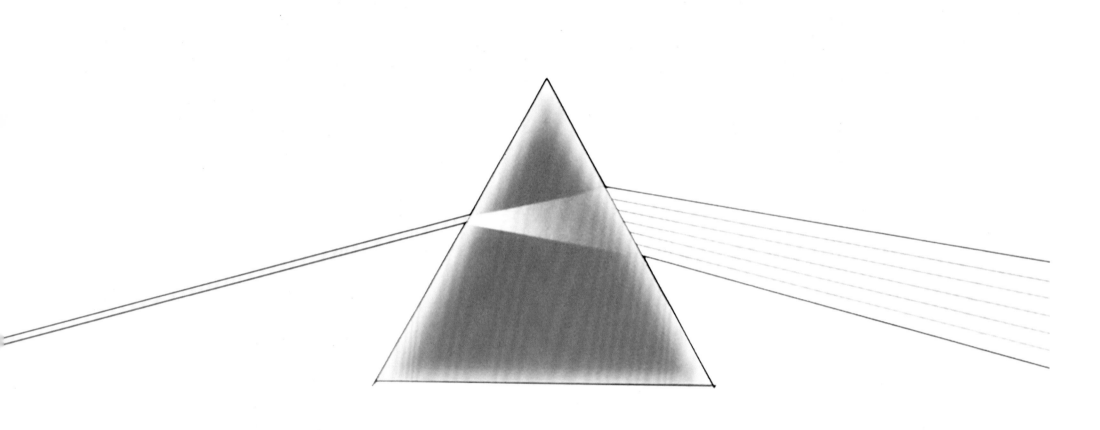

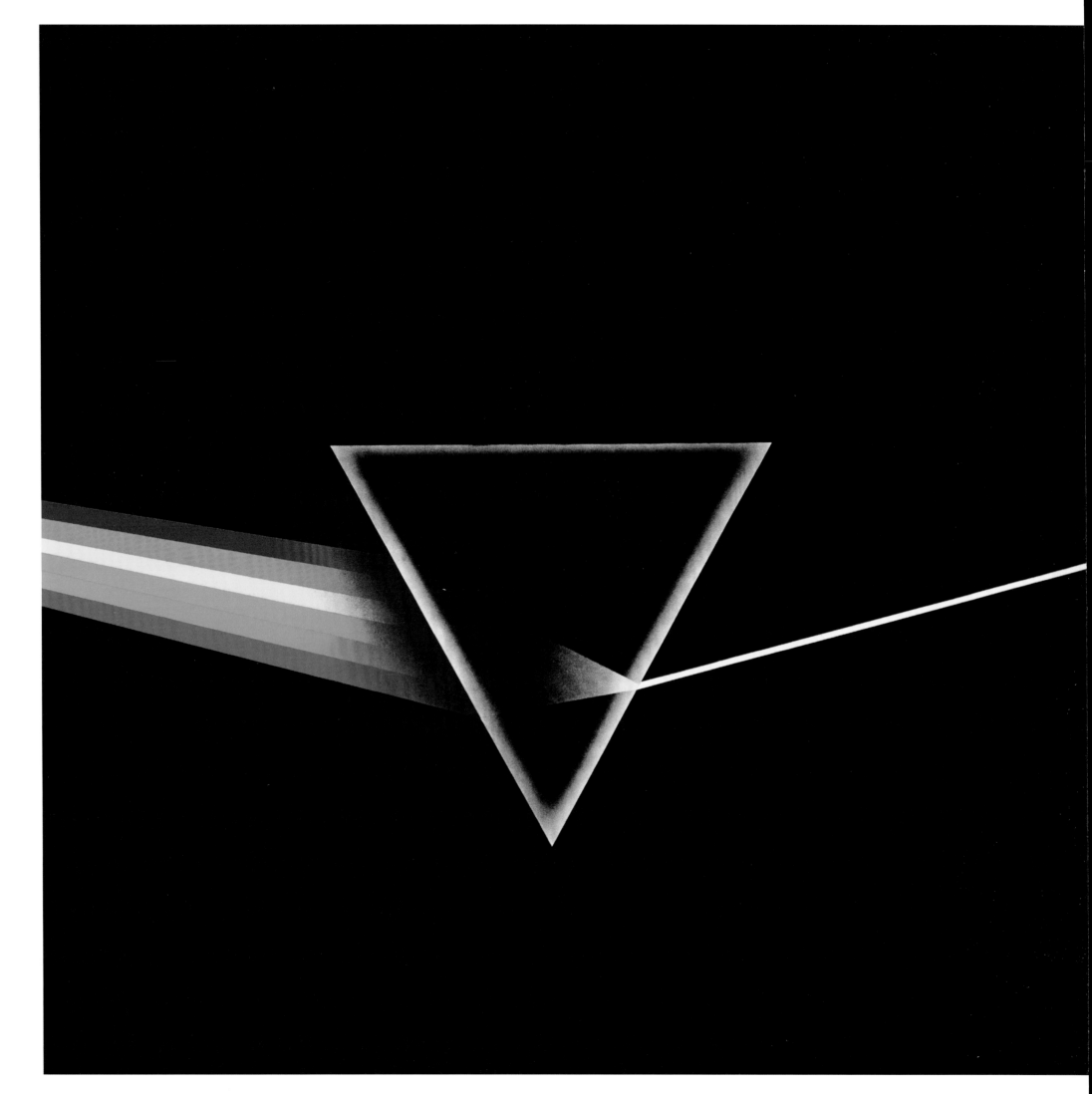

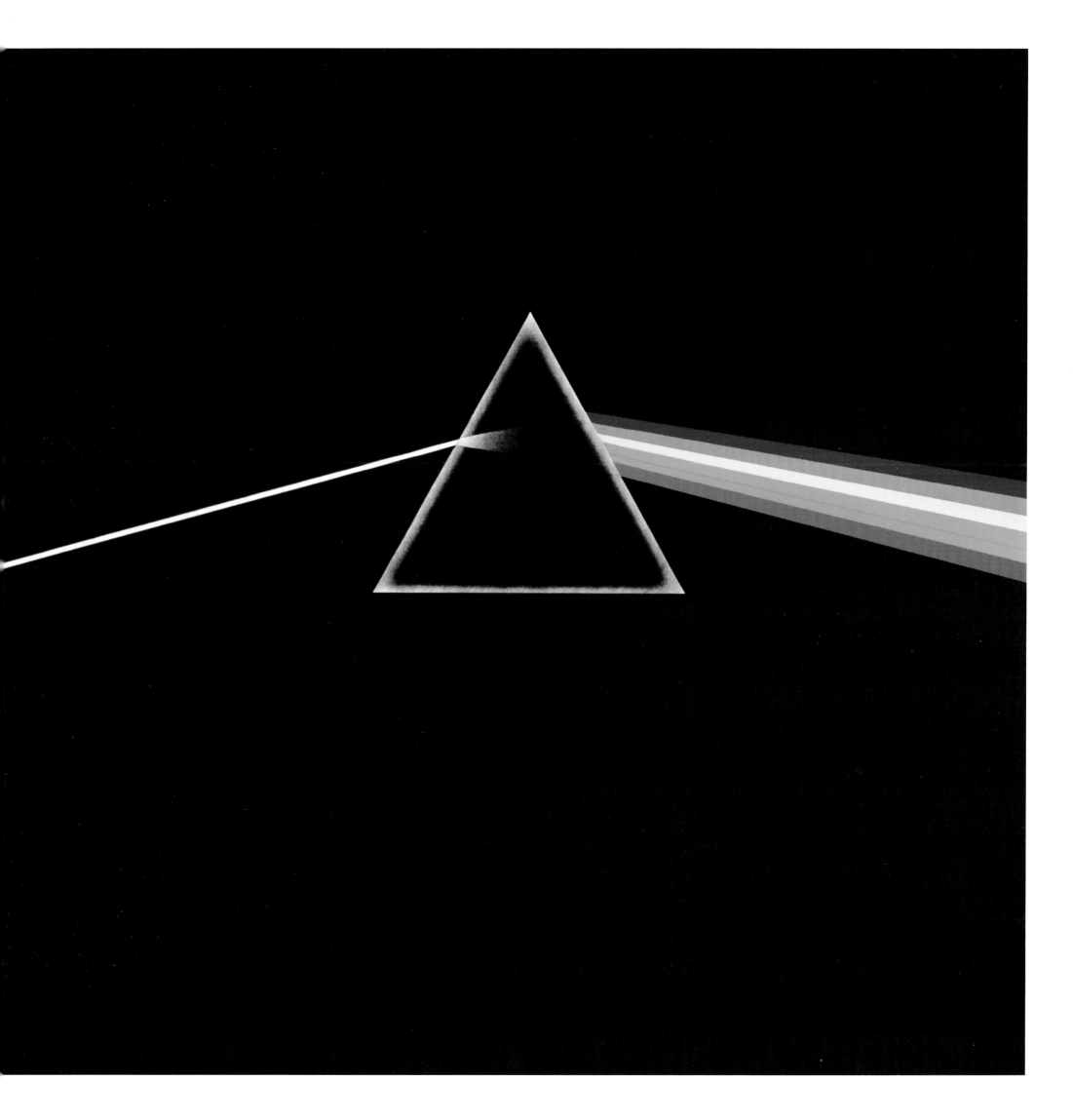

PINK FLOYD

INSIDE COVER
ALL BACKGROUND UP TO KEYLINES ⊘ PRINT SOLID BLACK. BLACK + 80% CYAN
DROP IN SIX COLOUR TINTS AS SHOWN ON THIS OVERLAY.

✱ NO KEYLINES TO APPEAR.

USE THE SAME SIX COLOUR TINTS FOR FRONT & BACK COVER.

SIDE ONE
1 SPEAK TO ME (Mason)
2 BREATHE (Waters, Gilmour, Wright)
3 ON THE RUN (Gilmour, Waters)
4 TIME (Mason, Waters, Wright, Gilmour)
5 THE GREAT GIG IN THE SKY (Wright)

SIDE TWO
1 MONEY (Waters)
2 US AND THEM (Waters, Wright)
3 ANY COLOUR YOU LIKE (Gilmour, Mason, Wright)
4 BRAIN DAMAGE (Waters)
5 ECLIPSE (waters)

DAVID GILMOUR Vocals, Guitars, VCS3
NICK MASON Percussion, Tape Effects
RICHARD WRIGHT Keyboards, Vocals, VCS3
ROGER WATERS Bass Guitar, Vocals, VCS3, Tape Effects

BREATHE

Breathe, breathe in the air
Don't be afraid to care
Leave, don't leave me
Walk around and choose your own ground
Long you live and high you fly
Smiles you'll give and tears you'll cry
All you touch and all you see
Is all your life will ever be

Run, rabbit, run
Dig that hole, forget the sun
And when at last the work is done
Don't sit down it's time to dig another one
For long you'll live, and high you'll fly
But only if you ride the tide
And balanced on the biggest wave
You race towards an early grave.

TIME

Ticking away the moments that make up a dull day
Fritter and waste the hours in an offhand way
Kicking around on a piece of ground in your hometown
Waiting for someone or something to show you the way

Tired of lying in the sunshine, staying home to watch the rain
You are young and life is long, and there is time to kill today
And then one day you find ten years have got behind you
No one told you when to run, you missed the starting gun

And you run, and you run to catch up with the sun but it's sinking
Racing around to come up behind you again
The sun is the same in a relative way but you're older
Shorter of breath and one day closer to death

Every year is getting shorter, never seem to find the time
Plans that either come to naught or half a page of scribbled lines
Hanging on in quiet desperation is the English way
The time is gone, the song is over, thought I'd something more to say

Breathe Reprise

Home, home again
I like to be here when I can
And when I come home cold and tired
It's good to warm my bones beside the fire
Far away across the field
The tolling of the iron bell
Calls the faithful to their knees
To hear the softly spoken magic spells.

MONEY

Money, Get away
Get a good job with more pay and you're O.K.
Money, it's a gas
Grab that cash with both hands and make a stash
New car, caviar, four star daydream
Think I'll buy me a football team

Money, get back
I'm alright Jack, keep your hands off of my stack
Money, it's a hit
Don't give me that do goody good bullshit
I'm in the hi-fidelity first class traveling set
And I think I need a Lear jet

Money, it's a crime
Share it fairly, but don't take a slice of my pie
Money, so they say
Is the root of all evil today
But if you ask for a rise it's no surprise that they're
giving none away

Produced by PINK FLOYD
Recorded at Abbey Road Studios, London
between June 1972 and January 1973

Engineer Alan Parsons
Assistant Peter James
Mixing Supervised by Chris Thomas

Saxophone on 'Us and Them' and 'Money' by Dick Parry

Vocals on 'The Great Gig in the Sky' by Clare Torry
Backing Vocals Doris Troy,
Leslie Duncan, Liza Strike, Barry St John

Sleeve Design by Hipgnosis
Sleeve Art by George Hardie N.T.A.
Photography buy Hipgnosis
Stickers Art by George Hardie N.T.A.

All lyrics by ROGER WATERS

℗ 1973 Also available on cassette and cartridge

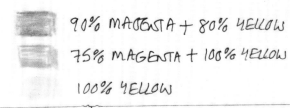

90% MAGENTA + 80% YELLOW

75% MAGENTA + 100% YELLOW

100% YELLOW

70% CYAN + 20% MAGENTA + 100% YELLOW

90% CYAN + 25% MAGENTA + 15% YELLOW

70% CYAN + 80% MAGENTA

REVERSE ALL CREDITS,
TRACK LIST & LYRICS TO
WHITE OUT OF SOLID BLACK

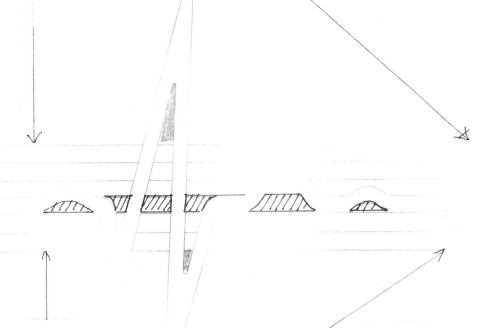

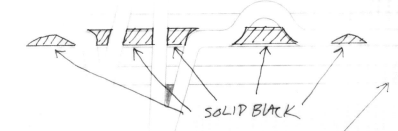

SOLID BLACK

US AND THEM

Us, and them
And after all we're only ordinary men
Me, and you
God only knows
It's not what we would choose to do
Forward he cried from the rear
And the front rank died
And the General sat, and the lines on the map
moved from side to side
Black and blue
And who knows which is which and who is who
Up and Down
And in the end it's only round and round and round
Haven't you heard it's a battle of words
the poster bearer cried
Listen son, said the man with the gun
There's room for you inside

Down and Out
It can't be helped but there's a lot of it about
With, without
And who'll deny it's what the fighting's all about
Out of the way, it's a busy day
I've got things on my mind
For the want of the price of tea and a slice
The old man died

BRAIN DAMAGE

The lunatic is on the grass
The lunatic is on the grass
Remembering games and daisy chains and laughs
Got to keep the loonies on the path

The lunatic is in the hall
The lunatics are in my hall
The paper holds their folded faces to the floor
And every day the paper boy brings more

And if the dam breaks open many years too soon
And if there is no room upon the hill
And if your head explodes with dark forebodings too
I'll see you on the dark side of the moon

The lunatic is in my head
The lunatic is in my head
You raise the blade, you make the change
You re-arrange me 'til I'm sane

You lock the door
And throw away the key
There's someone in my head but it's not me.

And if the cloud bursts, thunder in your ear
You shout and no one seems to hear
And if the band you're in starts playing different tunes
I'll see you on the dark side of the moon

ECLIPSE

All that you touch
And all that you see
All that you taste
All you feel
And all that you love
And all that you hate
All you distrust
All you save
All that you give
All that you deal
All that you buy
beg, borrow or steal
All you create
All you destroy
All that you do
All that you say
All that you eat
everyone you meet
All that you slight
everyone you fight
All that is now
All that is gone
All that's to come
and everything under the sun is in tune
but the sun is eclipsed by the moon.

SIDE ONE
1 SPEAK TO ME (Mason)
2 BREATHE (Waters, Gilmour, Wright)
3 ON THE RUN (Gilmour, Waters)
4 TIME (Mason, Waters, Wright, Gilmour)
5 THE GREAT GIG IN THE SKY (Wright)

SIDE TWO
1 MONEY (Waters)
2 US AND THEM (Waters, Wright)
3 ANY COLOUR YOU LIKE (Gilmour, Mason, Wright)
4 BRAIN DAMAGE (Waters)
5 ECLIPSE (Waters)

DAVID GILMOUR Vocals, Guitars, VCS3
NICK MASON Percussion, Tape Effects
RICHARD WRIGHT Keyboards, Vocals, VCS3
ROGER WATERS Bass Guitar, Vocals, VCS3, Tape Effects

BREATHE

Breathe, breathe in the air
Don't be afraid to care
Leave but don't leave me
Look around and choose your own ground
For long you live and high you fly
And smiles you'll give and tears you'll cry
And all you touch and all you see
Is all your life will ever be

Run rabbit run
Dig that hole, forget the sun,
And when at last the work is done
Don't sit down it's time to start another one
For long you live and high you fly
But only if you ride the tide
And balanced on the biggest wave
You race toward an early grave.

TIME

Ticking away the moments that make up a dull day
You fritter and waste the hours in an off hand way
Kicking around on a piece of ground in your home town
Waiting for someone or something to show you the way

Tired of lying in the sunshine staying home to watch the rain
You are young and life is long and there is time to kill today
And then one day you find ten years have got behind you
No one told you when to run, you missed the starting gun

And you run and you run to catch up with the sun, but it's sinking
And racing around to come up behind you again
The sun is the same in the relative way, but you're older
Shorter of breath and one day closer to death

Every year is getting shorter, never seem to find the time
Plans that either come to naught or half a page of scribbled lines
Hanging on in quiet desperation is the English way
The time is gone the song is over, thought I'd something more to say

Breathe Reprise

Home, home again
I like to be here when I can
When I come home cold and tired
It's good to warm my bones beside the fire
Far away across the field
The tolling of the iron bell
Calls the faithful to their knees
To hear the softly spoken magic spells.

MONEY

Money, get away
Get a good job with more pay and your O.K.
Money it's a gas
Grab that cash with both hands and make a stash
New car, caviar, four star daydream,
Think I'll buy me a football team

Money get back
I'm all right Jack keep your hands of my stack.
Money it's a hit
Don't give me that do goody good bullshit
I'm in the hi-fidelity first class travelling set
And I think I need a Lear jet

Money it's a crime
Share it fairly but don't take a slice of my pie
Money so they say
Is the root of all evil today
But if you ask for a rise it's no surprise that they're
giving none away

This STEREO record can be played on mono reproducers
provided either a compatible or stereo cartridge wired for
mono is fitted. Recent equipment may already be fitted
with a suitable cartridge. If in doubt consult your dealer.

E.M.I RECORDS (The Gramophone Company Ltd)
HAYES · MIDDLESEX · ENGLAND

Regd. Trade Mark
of The Gramophone
Company Ltd.
A COMPANY OF
THE EMI GROUP

Made and printed in the EU
File under POPULAR : Pop Groups

7303   TPS   SHVL 804

Produced by PINK FLOYD
Recorded at Abbey Road Studios, London
between June 1972 and January 1973

Engineer Alan Parsons
Assistant Peter James
Mixing Supervised by Chris Thomas

Saxophone on 'Us and Them' and 'Money' Dick Parry

Vocals on 'The Great Gig in the Sky' by Clare Torry
Backing Vocals Doris Troy,
Leslie Duncan, Liza Strike, Barry St John

Sleeve Design by Hipgnosis
Sleeve Art by George Hardie N.T.A.
Photography by Hipgnosis
Stickers Art by George Hardie N.T.A.

All lyrics by ROGER WATERS.

US AND THEM

Us, and them
And after all we're only ordinary men
Me, and you
God only knows it's not what we would choose to do
Forward he cried from the rear
and the front rank died
And the General sat, and the lines on the map
moved from side to side
Black and blue
And who knows which is which and who is who
Up and Down
And in the end it's only round and round and round
Haven't you heard it's a battle of words
the poster bearer cried
Listen son, said the man with the gun
There's room for you inside

Down and Out
It can't be helped but there's a lot of it about
With, without
And who'll deny it's what the fighting's all about
Out of the way, it's a busy day
I've got things on my mind
For want of the price of tea and a slice
The old man died

BRAIN DAMAGE

The lunatic is on the grass
The lunatic is on the grass
Remembering games and daisy chains and laughs
Got to keep the loonies on the path

The lunatic is in the hall
The lunatics are in my hall
The paper holds their folded faces to the floor
And every day the paper boy brings more

And if the dam breaks open many years too soon
And if there is no room upon the hill
And if your head explodes with dark forbodings too
I'll see you on the dark side of the moon

The lunatic is in my head
The lunatic is in my head
You raise the blade, you make the change
You re-arrange me 'till I'm sane

You lock the door
And throw away the key
There's someone in my head but it's not me.

And if the cloud bursts, thunder in your ear
You shout and no one seems to hear
And if the band you're in starts playing different tunes
I'll see you on the dark side of the moon.

ECLIPSE

All that you touch
All that you see
All that you taste
All you feel
All that you love
All that you hate
All you distrust
All you save
All that you give
All that you deal
All that you buy
beg, borrow or steal
All you create
All you destroy
All that you do
All that you say
All that you eat
everyone you meet
All that you slight
everyone you fight
All that is now
All that is gone
All that's to come
and everything under the sun is in tune
but the sun is eclipsed by the moon.

46   NOVEMBRE 1974, *Roger Waters, Nick Mason* et *Arthur Max*, concepteur de l'éclairage, à la console de mixage pendant un test de son, au Wembley Empire Pool, Londres, Royaume-Uni.
Archives de Jill Furmanovsky

47   NOVEMBRE 1974, *Richard Wright* et *Arthur Max*, concepteur de l'éclairage, à la console de mixage pendant un test de son, au Wembley Empire Pool, Londres, Royaume-Uni.
Archives de Jill Furmanovsky

48   NOVEMBRE 1974, *David Gilmour* et *Phil Taylor*, responsable technique des guitares, pendant un test de son, au Wembley Empire Pool, Londres, Royaume-Uni.
Archives de Jill Furmanovsky

49   NOVEMBRE 1974, *Roger Waters, Nick Mason* et *Richard Wright* pendant un test de son, au Empire Theatre, Liverpool, Royaume-Uni.
Storm Thorgerson et Aubrey « Po » Powell, Hipgnosis, Pink Floyd Music Ltd

50   DÉCEMBRE 1974, *David Gilmour* et *Roger Waters* pendant un test de son, à l'Hippodrome, Birmingham, Royaume-Uni.
Archives de Jill Furmanovsky

51   DÉCEMBRE 1974, *Nick Mason, David Gilmour* et *Roger Waters* pendant un test de son, à l'Hippodrome, Birmingham, Royaume-Uni.
Archives de Jill Furmanovsky

52   AVRIL 1975, *Roger Waters*, le directeur de production *Robbie Williams*, l'ingénieur du son *Brian Humphries* et l'intégrateur de systèmes de son *Bill Kelsey* pendant un test de son, au Pacific Coliseum, Vancouver, Canada.
Storm Thorgerson et Aubrey « Po » Powell, Hipgnosis, Pink Floyd Music Ltd

53   NOVEMBRE 1974, la choriste *Venetta Fields* lisant le programme *comic book* « Floyd » pendant un test de son, au Usher Hall, Édimbourg, Royaume-Uni.
Archives de Jill Furmanovsky

54   AVRIL 1975, test de son, au Los Angeles Memorial Sports Arena, États-Unis.
Storm Thorgerson et Aubrey « Po » Powell, Hipgnosis, Pink Floyd Music Ltd

55   NOVEMBRE 1974, test de son, au Usher Hall, Édimbourg, Royaume-Uni.
Archives de Jill Furmanovsky

56   DÉCEMBRE 1974, équipe de tournée, rangée avant: *Paul Devine, Pete Revell, Bernie Caulder, Paul Murray*, le second

technicien *Mick Kluczynski*, un inconnu, le responsable technique des guitares *Phil Taylor* et un inconnu; rangée arrière: *Graeme Fleming, Coon Thompson*, le directeur de production *Robbie Williams*, un inconnu, *Nick Rochford, Mick Marshall* et des inconnus, au Palace Theatre, Manchester, Royaume-Uni.
Archives de Pink Floyd

57   AVRIL 1975, des fans de Pink Floyd arrivant, au Pacific Coliseum, Vancouver, Canada.
Storm Thorgerson et Aubrey « Po » Powell, Hipgnosis, Pink Floyd Music Ltd

SPECTACLES

59   AVRIL 1975, des fans de Pink Floyd, au Los Angeles Memorial Sports Arena, États-Unis.
Storm Thorgerson et Aubrey « Po » Powell, Hipgnosis, Pink Floyd Music Ltd

60   JUIN 1972, *Roger Waters* en spectacle, au Dome, Brighton, Royaume-Uni.
Archives de Jill Furmanovsky

61   JUIN 1972, *David Gilmour, Nick Mason* et *Roger Waters* en spectacle, au Dome, Brighton, Royaume-Uni.
Archives de Jill Furmanovsky

62   AVRIL 1975, le groupe en spectacle, jeux d'éclairage et effet de brouillard avec de la glace sèche, au Pacific Coliseum, Vancouver, Canada.
Storm Thorgerson et Aubrey « Po » Powell, Hipgnosis, Pink Floyd Music Ltd

63   MAI 1973, le groupe en spectacle, jeux d'éclairage et effet de brouillard avec de la glace sèche, au Earls Court, Londres, Royaume-Uni.
Archives de Jill Furmanovsky

64   OCTOBRE 1972, le groupe en spectacle, jeux d'éclairage et effet de brouillard avec de la glace sèche, au Wembley Empire Pool, Londres, Royaume-Uni.
Archives de Jill Furmanovsky

65   NOVEMBRE 1974, des fans de Pink Floyd, au Wembley Empire Pool, Londres, Royaume-Uni.
Archives de Jill Furmanovsky

66   MAI 1973, le groupe en spectacle, au Earls Court, Londres, Royaume-Uni.
Archives de Jill Furmanovsky

67   NOVEMBRE 1974, *David Gilmour* jouant de la *steel guitar* électrique Jedson, au Empire Theatre, Liverpool, Royaume-Uni.
Archives de Jill Furmanovsky

68   NOVEMBRE 1973, *Roger Waters* en spectacle, au Rainbow Theatre, Londres, Royaume-Uni.
Archives de Jill Furmanovsky

69   NOVEMBRE 1973, les choristes *Vicki Brown, Liza Strike* et *Clare Torry* en spectacle, au Rainbow Theatre, Londres, Royaume-Uni.
Archives de Jill Furmanovsky

70   NOVEMBRE 1974, *Richard Wright* en spectacle, au Wembley Empire Pool, Londres, Royaume-Uni.
Archives de Jill Furmanovsky

71   NOVEMBRE 1973, *Nick Mason* en spectacle, au Rainbow Theatre, Londres, Royaume-Uni.
Archives de Jill Furmanovsky

72   AVRIL 1975, le groupe en spectacle, au Pacific Coliseum, Vancouver, Canada.
Storm Thorgerson et Aubrey « Po » Powell, Hipgnosis, Pink Floyd Music Ltd

73   MAI 1973, *Roger Waters* en spectacle et un gong enflammé, au Earls Court, Londres, Royaume-Uni.
Archives de Jill Furmanovsky

74   NOVEMBRE 1974, des fans de Pink Floyd, au Wembley Empire Pool, Londres, Royaume-Uni.
Storm Thorgerson et Aubrey « Po » Powell, Hipgnosis, Pink Floyd Music Ltd

75   MAI 1973, *David Gilmour* en spectacle, au Earls Court, Londres, Royaume-Uni.
Archives de Jill Furmanovsky

76   NOVEMBRE 1974, le groupe en spectacle et projection sur écran, au Empire Theatre, Liverpool, Royaume-Uni.
Storm Thorgerson et Aubrey « Po » Powell, Hipgnosis, Pink Floyd Music Ltd

77   NOVEMBRE 1974, *David Gilmour, Nick Mason* et *Roger Waters* en spectacle et projection sur écran, au Wembley Empire Pool, Londres, Royaume-Uni.
Archives de Jill Furmanovsky

78   DÉCEMBRE 1974, *Nick Mason* et *Roger Waters* en spectacle et projection sur écran, au Palace Theatre, Manchester, Royaume-Uni.
Archives de Jill Furmanovsky

79   DÉCEMBRE 1974, projection d'une animation créée par *Ian Emes* pour accompagner la chanson *Time*, au Palace Theatre, Manchester, Royaume-Uni.
Archives de Jill Furmanovsky

80   AVRIL 1975, le groupe en spectacle devant l'écran de projection, au Pacific

Coliseum, Vancouver, Canada.
Storm Thorgerson et Aubrey « Po » Powell, Hipgnosis, Pink Floyd Music Ltd

81   AVRIL 1975, *Nick Mason* en spectacle, au Pacific Coliseum, Vancouver, Canada.
Storm Thorgerson et Aubrey « Po » Powell, Hipgnosis, Pink Floyd Music Ltd

82   AVRIL 1975, les choristes *Venetta Fields* et *Carlena Williams* en spectacle, au Los Angeles Memorial Sports Arena, États-Unis.
Storm Thorgerson et Aubrey « Po » Powell, Hipgnosis, Pink Floyd Music Ltd

83   NOVEMBRE 1974, *Roger Waters* en spectacle, au Usher Hall, Édimbourg, Royaume-Uni.
Archives de Jill Furmanovsky

84   NOVEMBRE 1974, *David Gilmour* en spectacle, au Wembley Empire Pool, Londres, Royaume-Uni.
Archives de Jill Furmanovsky

85   AVRIL 1975, *Richard Wright* en spectacle, au Pacific Coliseum, Vancouver, Canada.
Storm Thorgerson et Aubrey « Po » Powell, Hipgnosis, Pink Floyd Music Ltd

86   DÉCEMBRE 1974, les choristes *Venetta Fields* et *Carlena Williams* en spectacle, au Palace Theatre, Manchester, Royaume-Uni.
Archives de Jill Furmanovsky

87   NOVEMBRE 1974, *Nick Mason* en spectacle, au Empire Pool, Wembley, Royaume-Uni.
Archives de Jill Furmanovsky

88   NOVEMBRE 1974, *Roger Waters* en spectacle, au Wembley Empire Pool, Londres, Royaume-Uni.
Archives de Jill Furmanovsky

89   AVRIL 1975, la choriste *Carlena Williams* en spectacle, au Los Angeles Memorial Sports Arena, États-Unis.
Storm Thorgerson et Aubrey « Po » Powell, Hipgnosis, Pink Floyd Music Ltd

90   DÉCEMBRE 1974, des fans de Pink Floyd, au Palace Theatre, Manchester, Royaume-Uni.
Archives de Jill Furmanovsky

91   NOVEMBRE 1974, le groupe en spectacle et une reproduction d'avion s'apprêtant à s'écraser sur scène, au Wembley Empire Pool, Londres, Royaume-Uni.
Archives de Jill Furmanovsky

92   AVRIL 1975, *Nick Mason* jouant sur sa batterie Ludwig ornée de l'œuvre

« Hokusai Wave » peinte à la main par *Kate Hepburn*, au Los Angeles Memorial Sports Arena, États-Unis.
Storm Thorgerson et Aubrey « Po » Powell, Hipgnosis, Pink Floyd Music Ltd

93   AVRIL 1975, *David Gilmour* jouant de la *steel guitar*, au Los Angeles Memorial Sports Arena, États-Unis.
Storm Thorgerson et Aubrey « Po » Powell, Hipgnosis, Pink Floyd Music Ltd

94   AVRIL 1975, *David Gilmour* et *Richard Wright* en spectacle, au Pacific Coliseum, Vancouver, Canada.
Storm Thorgerson et Aubrey « Po » Powell, Hipgnosis, Pink Floyd Music Ltd

95   AVRIL 1975, *Roger Waters* et *Richard Wright* en spectacle, au Los Angeles Memorial Sports Arena, États-Unis.
Storm Thorgerson et Aubrey « Po » Powell, Hipgnosis, Pink Floyd Music Ltd

96   AVRIL 1975, *Roger Waters* et *Richard Wright* en spectacle, au Los Angeles Memorial Sports Arena, États-Unis.
Storm Thorgerson et Aubrey « Po » Powell, Hipgnosis, Pink Floyd Music Ltd

97   AVRIL 1975, *Richard Wright* et *Roger Waters* en spectacle, au Pacific Coliseum, Vancouver, Canada.
Storm Thorgerson et Aubrey « Po » Powell, Hipgnosis, Pink Floyd Music Ltd

98   NOVEMBRE 1974, le groupe en spectacle et effets laser, au Wembley Empire Pool, Londres, États-Unis.
Archives de Jill Furmanovsky

99   NOVEMBRE 1974, des fans de Pink Floyd, au Usher Hall, Édimbourg, Royaume-Uni.
Archives de Jill Furmanovsky

100   NOVEMBRE 1974, *Nick Mason* en spectacle, au Usher Hall, Édimbourg, Royaume-Uni.
Archives de Jill Furmanovsky

101   AVRIL 1975, *Roger Waters* en spectacle, au Pacific Coliseum, Vancouver, Canada.
Storm Thorgerson et Aubrey « Po » Powell, Hipgnosis, Pink Floyd Music Ltd

102   JUIN 1972, *David Gilmour* en spectacle, au Dome, Brighton, Royaume-Uni.
Archives de Jill Furmanovsky

103   AVRIL 1975, *Richard Wright* en spectacle, au Tucson Community Center, Arizona, États-Unis.
Storm Thorgerson et Aubrey « Po » Powell, Hipgnosis, Pink Floyd Music Ltd

104   DÉCEMBRE 1974, *David Gilmour*, *Nick Mason* et *Roger Waters* en spectacle, au Palace Theatre, Manchester, Royaume-Uni.
Archives de Jill Furmanovsky

105   DÉCEMBRE 1974, *Roger Waters* et le saxophoniste *Dick Parry* en spectacle, au Palace Theatre, Manchester, Royaume-Uni.
Archives de Jill Furmanovsky

106   DÉCEMBRE 1974, *David Gilmour*, en spectacle, à l'Hippodrome, Birmingham, Royaume-Uni.
Archives de Jill Furmanovsky

107   NOVEMBRE 1974, *Roger Waters* en spectacle, au Usher Hall, Édimbourg, Royaume-Uni.
Archives de Jill Furmanovsky

108   DÉCEMBRE 1974, *Roger Waters* et *David Gilmour* en spectacle, à l'Hippodrome, Birmingham, Royaume-Uni.
Archives de Jill Furmanovsky

109   NOVEMBRE 1974, *Richard Wright*, *Roger Waters*, *Nick Mason* et *David Gilmour* en spectacle, au Wembley Empire Pool, Londres, Royaume-Uni.
Storm Thorgerson et Aubrey « Po » Powell, Hipgnosis, Pink Floyd Music Ltd

110   NOVEMBRE 1974, *Nick Mason* en spectacle, au Wembley Empire Pool, Londres, Royaume-Uni.
Archives de Jill Furmanovsky

111   AVRIL 1975, *Richard Wright* en spectacle, au Los Angeles Memorial Sports Arena, États-Unis.
Storm Thorgerson et Aubrey « Po » Powell, Hipgnosis, Pink Floyd Music Ltd

112   NOVEMBRE 1974, *David Gilmour* et les choristes *Venetta Fields* et *Carlena Williams* en spectacle et jeux d'éclairage, au Wembley Empire Pool, Londres, Royaume-Uni.
Archives de Jill Furmanovsky

113   NOVEMBRE 1974, le groupe en spectacle, au Empire Theatre, Liverpool, Royaume-Uni.
Archives de Jill Furmanovsky

114   NOVEMBRE 1974, des fans de Pink Floyd, au Wembley Empire Pool, Londres, Royaume-Uni.
Archives de Jill Furmanovsky

115   NOVEMBRE 1974, projection sur écran, au Wembley Empire Pool, Londres, Royaume-Uni.
Archives de Jill Furmanovsky

116   NOVEMBRE 1974, *Roger Waters* sur scène, au Wembley Empire Pool, Londres, Royaume-Uni.
Storm Thorgerson et Aubrey « Po » Powell, Hipgnosis, Pink Floyd Music Ltd

117   NOVEMBRE 1974, des fans de Pink Floyd formant des pyramides avec leurs mains, au Wembley Empire Pool, Londres, Royaume-Uni.
Storm Thorgerson et Aubrey « Po » Powell, Hipgnosis, Pink Floyd Music Ltd

118   AVRIL 1975, après le spectacle, au Los Angeles Memorial Sports Arena, États-Unis.
Storm Thorgerson et Aubrey « Po » Powell, Hipgnosis, Pink Floyd Music Ltd

HORS SCÈNE

120   DÉCEMBRE 1974, *Nick Mason*, *Roger Waters*, la choriste *Carlena Williams*, le responsable technique des guitares *Phil Taylor* et d'autres membres de l'équipe de tournée, dans un bar, après un spectacle au Palace Theatre, Manchester, Royaume-Uni.
Archives de Jill Furmanovsky

121   DÉCEMBRE 1974, *David Gilmour* et les choristes *Carlena Williams* et *Venetta Fields* dans un bar, après un spectacle au Palace Theatre, Manchester, Royaume-Uni.
Archives de Jill Furmanovsky

122   DÉCEMBRE 1974, *David Gilmour*, *Roger Waters* et le designer de l'album chez Hipgnosis *Storm Thorgerson* dans un bar, après un spectacle au Palace Theatre, Manchester, Royaume-Uni.
Archives de Jill Furmanovsky

123   DÉCEMBRE 1974, *Roger Waters* et le designer de l'album chez Hipgnosis *Storm Thorgerson* dans un bar, après un spectacle au Palace Theatre, Manchester, Royaume-Uni.
Archives de Jill Furmanovsky

124   AVRIL 1975, *Richard Wright* à une station de ski, un jour de tournée au Pacific Coliseum, Vancouver, Canada.
Storm Thorgerson et Aubrey « Po » Powell, Hipgnosis, Pink Floyd Music Ltd

125   AVRIL 1975, *David Gilmour* à une station de ski, un jour de tournée au Pacific Coliseum, Vancouver, Canada.
Storm Thorgerson et Aubrey « Po » Powell, Hipgnosis, Pink Floyd Music Ltd

126   DÉCEMBRE 1974, *Nick Mason* et *Richard Wright* à un club de sports, pendant les jours de tournée à l'Hippodrome, Birmingham,

Royaume-Uni.
Archives de Jill Furmanovsky

127   DÉCEMBRE 1974, *David Gilmour*
et *Richard Wright*, lisant les journaux
The Sun et le *Daily Mirror* à un club de
sports, pendant les jours de tournée à
l'Hippodrome, Birmingham,
Royaume-Uni.
Archives de Jill Furmanovsky

128   DÉCEMBRE 1974, *Roger Waters* et
Nick Sedgwick, un ami du groupe, jouant
une ronde de golf pendant les jours de
tournée au Palace Theatre, Manchester,
Royaume-Uni.
Archives de Jill Furmanovsky

129   DÉCEMBRE 1974, *David Gilmour*,
Roger Waters et le designer de l'album
chez Hipgnosis *Storm Thorgerson*
jouant au squash à un club de sports,
pendant les jours de tournée à
l'Hippodrome, Birmingham,
Royaume-Uni.
Storm Thorgerson et *Aubrey « Po » Powell*,
Hipgnosis, Pink Floyd Music Ltd

130   DÉCEMBRE 1974, *Roger Waters*
jouant au squash à un club de sports,
pendant les jours de tournée à
l'Hippodrome, Birmingham,
Royaume-Uni.
Storm Thorgerson et *Aubrey « Po » Powell*,
Hipgnosis, Pink Floyd Music Ltd

131   NOVEMBRE 1974, *Richard Wright*
jouant au squash à un club de sports,
pendant les jours de tournée au Usher
Hall, Édimbourg, Royaume-Uni.
Archives de Jill Furmanovsky

132   NOVEMBRE 1974, *David Gilmour*
jouant au squash à un club de sports,
pendant les jours de tournée au Usher
Hall, Édimbourg, Royaume-Uni.
Archives de Jill Furmanovsky

133   NOVEMBRE 1974, *David Gilmour*
et *Nick Mason* jouant au squash à
un club de sports, pendant les jours de
tournée au Usher Hall, Édimbourg,
Royaume-Uni.
Archives de Jill Furmanovsky

134   DÉCEMBRE 1974, *Nick Mason* dans
une voiture-restaurant à bord d'un train
vers Birmingham, Royaume-Uni, pendant
le British Winter Tour.
Archives de Jill Furmanovsky

135   DÉCEMBRE 1974, *Roger Waters*,
l'ingénieur de son *Brian Humphries* et le
directeur de tournée *Warwick McCredie*
à bord d'un train vers Birmingham,
Royaume-Uni, pendant le British
Winter Tour.
Archives de Jill Furmanovsky

136   DÉCEMBRE 1974, la photographe de
rock *Jill Furmanovsky* à bord d'un train
vers Birmingham, Royaume-Uni, pendant
le British Winter Tour.
Archives de Jill Furmanovsky

137   DÉCEMBRE 1974, *Roger Waters*
et *Nick Mason* à bord d'un train vers
Birmingham, Royaume-Uni, pendant le
British Winter Tour.
Archives de Jill Furmanovsky

138   NOVEMBRE 1974, *David Gilmour*,
la photographe de rock *Jill Furmanovsky*
et l'ami du groupe *Nick Sedgwick* à bord
d'un train vers Birmingham, Royaume-
Uni, pendant le British Winter Tour.
Storm Thorgerson et *Aubrey « Po » Powell*,
Hipgnosis, Pink Floyd Music Ltd

139   NOVEMBRE 1974, *David Gilmour*,
le directeur de tournée *Warwick
McCredie*, la choriste *Carlena Williams*, le
saxophoniste *Dick Parry* et le designer de
l'album chez Hipgnosis *Storm Thorgerson*
(photographiant), qui arrivent à l'hôtel
avant un spectacle au Usher Hall,
Édimbourg, Royaume-Uni.
Archives de Jill Furmanovsky

140   NOVEMBRE 1974, *David Gilmour*,
Richard Wright et le designer de l'album
chez Hipgnosis *Storm Thorgerson* jouant
au backgammon dans une chambre
d'hôtel pendant les jours de tournée au
Usher Hall, Édimbourg, Royaume-Uni.
Archives de Jill Furmanovsky

141   NOVEMBRE 1974, *David Gilmour*,
Richard Wright et les designers de
l'album chez Hipgnosis *Aubrey « Po »
Powell* et *Storm Thorgerson*, pendant le
British Winter Tour.
Archives de Jill Furmanovsky

158   PINK FLOYD 1971, *Richard Wright,
Nick Mason, Roger Waters* et *David
Gilmour* dans Belsize Park, Londres,
Royaume-Uni.
Pink Floyd Music Ltd

159   PINK FLOYD 1971, *Richard Wright,
Nick Mason, Roger Waters* et *David
Gilmour* se cachant le visage, dans Belsize
Park, Londres, Royaume-Uni.
Pink Floyd Music Ltd

160   JANVIER 1972, publicité du *Melody
Maker* annonçant les dates de tournée de
Pink Floyd pour les deux premiers mois
de l'année.
Archives de Pink Floyd

Édition originale publiée au Royaume-Uni
par Thames & Hudson Ltd, 181A High
Holborn, Londres, sous le titre
*Pink Floyd The Dark Side Of The Moon
50th Anniversary*.

Pink Floyd The Dark Side Of The
Moon © 2023 Pink Floyd Music Ltd en
collaboration avec Thames & Hudson Ltd.

Photographies gracieuseté de Hipgnosis
Ltd © 2023 Pink Floyd Music Ltd et
Archives de Jill Furmanovsky.
Pour toutes les sources, voir les pages
154 à 157.

Dirigé par: JILL FURMANOVSKY

Direction artistique: AUBREY POWELL

Design graphique: Pentagram

Traitement des images: Tracey Kraft,
archives de Pink Floyd

Pour l'édition française:

Traduction: Clémence Risler,
Antoine Ross Trempe et Joëlle Landry

Révision: Marco Chioini

Adaptation: Karine Raymond et
Francis Lepage

Publié en français par:

Les Éditions Cardinal
7240, rue Saint-Hubert
Montréal, QC
CANADA H2R 2N1
editions-cardinal.ca

Pour la traduction française:
© 2023, Éditions Cardinal

ISBN 978-2-925078-91-3

Imprimé et relié en Italie

PINK FLOYD
TOUR '72

Jan.	20th	The Dome, Brighton
	21st	Guildhall, Portsmouth
	22nd	Winter Gardens, Bournemouth
	23rd	Guildhall, Southampton
	27th	City Hall, Newcastle
	28th	Town Hall, Leeds
Feb.	5th	Colston Hall, Bristol
	10th	De Montfort Hall, Leicester
	11th	Free Trade Hall, Manchester
	12th	City Hall, Sheffield
	13th	Empire, Liverpool

FEBRUARY 17th, 18th & 19th
RAINBOW THEATRE, LONDON